ARGUING A

ARGUING
ABOUT
CHRISTIANITY

seven discussions between

WILLIAM BARCLAY

and

IAIN REID

THE SAINT ANDREW PRESS
EDINBURGH

First published in 1980 by
THE SAINT ANDREW PRESS
121 George Street, Edinburgh EH2 4YN

Copyright © Iain Reid and
the estate of William Barclay 1980

ISBN 0 7152 0427 0

Printed in Great Britain by
Robert MacLehose and Co. Ltd.
Printers to the University of Glasgow

CONTENTS

FOREWORD

If ever a man loved an argument, it was my father. In *Who's Who*, he gave his two outside interests as 'music and arguments'. And whilst he loved music, he thrived on argument. He would often introduce a subject into our family conversations which he knew would have us all arguing frantically within a few minutes. Some of my happiest memories are of the Saturdays and Sundays when my wife, myself and my children used to go round to my parents' home, ostensibly for tea, but really for a good chat. In no time at all we would be discussing subjects which ranged from the meaning of Communion to the best way to prune roses. I have often heard my father change sides half-way through the argument and put his points just as convincingly! At other times he would stick stubbornly to his case when the facts were very much against him. He loved talking to people and people loved talking to him.

The wonderful thing about my father's arguments was that they destroyed no-one. He seemed to want to make people *think*, to stimulate his friends and his family to see another side of a subject. He would never hurt anyone in an argument but he would lead people till they saw for themselves the point he wanted them to see.

The one thing which worried him most was the closed mind. He loved to quote from Cromwell's letter to the General Assembly of the Church of Scotland: 'I beseech you, in the bowels of Christ, think it possible you may be mistaken.'

Sometimes my father trailed his coat blatantly, and there are indications of this in the interviews in this book. He would give an outrageous answer just to test you out. Not for one minute would I say that he was logical. He could conveniently forget the first part of a discussion, if he felt that the argument needed a new direction, and many is the time that our arguments went round in a full circle and we all finished up in fits of laughter. It was J. M. Barrie who said, 'Those who bring sunshine into the lives of others can't keep it from themselves' and often my father's sense of fun and gift for words brought sunshine and happiness into the lives of others, as the phenomenal sales of his books around the world show.

It is remarkable how clearly I can hear my father's voice through these interviews. I can hear him being very provocative, quite sharp now and again but then almost immediately kind and helpful. He loved to ask you questions. He could turn your questions round on you and I never ceased to marvel how he managed it. I can hear some of his favourite 'show stoppers', and the moments when we gasped and said 'You just must be joking!' There would be that twinkle in his eye and as we flung our combined arguments at him, he would sit there giving as good as he was getting. The only person who could really get the better of him at times like these was my mother. She would tell him in a very down-to-earth manner to stop talking nonsense, and for a moment or two we almost won the argument. These were wonderful days which brought the family close together and it all happened through the power of words and thoughts and argument. The interviews in this book give at least some idea of the kind of arguments in which my father delighted and the manner in which he loved to argue.

One of my father's favourite quotations runs like this:

> God give me sympathy and sense
> and help me keep my courage high.
> God give me calm and confidence
> and please—a twinkle in my eye.

In these interviews you will find the sympathy and the sense and all the other things, too. I just hope you do not miss that twinkle in his eye!

Ronnie Barclay

Discussion One

'Proof of God'

Reid: FOR me, there seems to be little real, conclusive evidence that there is a God. There seems only to be subjective evidence, an inner feeling concerning him. Is there more to it than that?

Barclay: I would like to say first of all that some people are natural believers and some people are natural doubters. I happen to belong to the natural believers. I never at any time really doubted my faith. Neither have I at any time thought it out. What you are challenging me to do is to think it out: is there any real evidence for the existence of God?

You've got the standard arguments. The oldest is the argument about *design*. It is Paley's famous argument about the watch: a man is crossing a moor and kicks his foot against a watch. He has never seen a watch in his life before. He picks it up. He examines it. He soon sees that it is made of porcelain, metal and steel and springs and cog wheels, all wound up and going in a certain predetermined order. What does he argue? Does he argue that all this steel and gold and porcelain and so on must have come from the ends of the earth, must have made themselves into a watch, must have wound themselves up and set themselves going? No, if he's got a natural kind of mind at all, he says, 'I've found a watch; somewhere there must be a watchmaker.'

The world is more accurate than any watch and, when applied to the world, the argument says, 'I have found a world. Somewhere there must be a world-maker, and that world-maker must be *mind*, for where there is order there must be mind. Order indicates mind and, of course, the world is full of order.'

That's the oldest argument.

Reid: Is it watertight?

Barclay: Not entirely. It is only fair to point out its big fault. If you find a watch, it's not an argument that there is a watchmaker, it's an argument that there has been a watchmaker. The argument, applied to the world, would not mean necessarily that there is a God but that, at some time or other, there was a God. A God who set it going.

Reid: That is a very ingenious argument. Are there other arguments for the existence of God that you would like to put forward?

Barclay: Well, there is the argument that there must be a first cause. In other words, you did something because something happened, and that thing happened because something else had previously happened, and so on. If you press back and back and back, there must have been some beginning to the whole thing, something that set the whole thing going. The Greeks used to call God 'the unmoved mover'. He himself wasn't moved, but he is the moving cause of everything. If you press far enough back, you get some initial cause, and you therefore come up with God. I think this one does make sense. But again, on the whole it presents you with a God who was, rather than a God who is, the starting point to the whole thing.

Reid: Well, is there any proof that God exists today, that God *is*?

Barclay: The proof really is this, that whatever you say about the world, it's not finished. The act of creation is still going on. It's still throwing out new things, new truths and new powers. Therefore, there seems to be some action taking place in it yet, and that action may well point to God.

Reid: Is this continuing creation which you have just indicated what some theologians call 'process theology'?

Barclay: Yes, in the ancient world, in the Bible for instance, writers often thought in terms of 'flashpoint theology': the world was created in a week, the last judgment will be in an hour, all this kind of thing. But the modern theologian thinks not so much of 'flashpoint theology' but, as you call it, 'process theology' (which I prefer to call 'dynamic theology') meaning that God is still acting, still creating, still judging; God judging all the time. It seems to me that there is evidence that God is still in action.

Reid: You said that God is 'mind'. Does this mean that the old image of the bearded man in the sky is now out?

Barclay: It's out technically, it's out academically, it's out theologically. But I question if it will ever be entirely out. Surely this is why the Incarnation was so necessary. I mean, because we are human beings, we cannot possibly think of God in any other way except as a person. And, when men thought of God as a person, they thought of him as a reverend, grave, old figure. They couldn't help doing that. I don't think that the ordinary person can think in terms of pure spirit at all. Can you?

Reid: I don't know if I can, but I certainly don't think of God as a figure of a man. I think of him as love, but that's a very abstract term.

Barclay: Even if you think of him as love, what shape is this love, so to speak? You need to think in terms of how this

4 *Arguing About Christianity*

love is embodied, and this, of course, is why we were given Jesus. Jesus came to let us see what God is like.

Reid: But I believe that God is everywhere. Therefore, if I believe that, how can I visualise him as a human figure? Such a figure would anchor him to one place at a time.

Barclay: I don't think visualising God as a person is necessarily something we set out to do. I think we do it because we have to. For example, suppose there's a person I haven't seen for years and years and years, and suppose that at one time I was very friendly with that person. Now, when I think of that person, I don't really think of his shape and his appearance, I think of the kind of attitude, the kind of spirit, the kind of atmosphere he created when we were together. I don't think so much of him as of what you might call the essence of the man. Well, I think that it's something like that with God. We think of the essence of God, but it's just that we who are human cannot really imagine any other way of acting than acting through the body. Therefore, we are very apt to make a figure of God in order to see him acting.

Reid: It's really impossible for us to try to begin to understand God, isn't it, because how can the created one understand the Creator?

Barclay: It is a point we must always remember that if you could understand God, he would cease to be God. By definition, he is beyond our understanding. And this again, I think, is why Jesus was so necessary. In Jesus the non-understandable becomes understandable, the unseeable becomes seeable. This is why he came into the world.

Reid: Christians say Jesus was the Incarnation. Does that rule out other incarnations? Are we not ourselves, in a sense, incarnations also?

Barclay: It doesn't rule out other incarnations in the basic sense of the term, but it does rule out anyone other than Jesus who is the full incarnation of God. In Jesus, we see God in his fullness. I agree with you that, in a sense, every man is an incarnation of God. After all, the Bible says that we're made in God's image and God's likeness—which is to say, in a way, that we are all incarnations of the God who made us. But not in the full sense, like Jesus.

Reid: Why do you suggest that there could never be another full incarnation? Surely God, if he wished, could repeat the process.

Barclay: There is a real sense in which the great things have only to be done once. The Greeks had a proverb, 'It cannot happen twice.' You can't have two Homers, you can't have two Aristotles, you can't have two Platos, you can't have two Shakespeares. The thing has happened; and it has happened once. And that, I think, is the case with the Incarnation. It happens once. If you had a series of incarnations of God, then you would unquestionably get a doubt as to what God was like. You'd be putting the one against the other and comparing them. When you have one perfect incarnation you really can say, 'I know what God is like.'

Reid: What is the evidence for saying that Jesus was the perfect incarnation of God? It seems to me that this is something we really cannot know. Only God can know that.

Barclay: Yes, but there's a certain amount of evidence. First, Jesus laid down an ethical teaching which is, to this day, accepted but which has never been fulfilled: he laid down an ethic which is the ideal ethic. Secondly, (and this brings in a side of the question which at the moment

we may not stop to look at), he clearly had powers which
the ordinary person didn't have. You *cannot* wipe out
Jesus' miracles. Thirdly, there is the argument which in
one sense is no argument but which in another sense is
the final argument—that of experience. Those who have
experienced the presence and the power of Jesus.

Reid: My view of Jesus, for what it is worth, is that he was a
man, in the normal sense of that word. He was a man
who, because he was able to surrender to God's power
and God's will, was able to act on earth, in a sense, as if
he were God. But he wasn't God. He was doing what
God would have him do. Where does that go off the
rails?

Barclay: It doesn't go off the rails altogether but it leaves a
good deal unexplained. Would you say, to re-phrase
your statement, that Jesus was the only person who ever
perfectly did the will of God? And would you say that he
became that rather than was that?

Reid: Yes.

Barclay: All this I would agree with. But you would then
have to ask, 'How did he manage to do it?' And you
would also have to ask, 'How did he manage to have the
colossal effect on other people that he seems to have
had?' You can't explain Jesus only in human terms, it
seems to me. Certainly he was a man, and I don't think
he had any qualifications of manhood that we haven't
got. If he had, he was cheating. You can't say he's an
example to us and then say he had all kinds of special
advantages. No, I think he was quite definitely a man just
as you and I are men. But I don't think you can simply
say that this man came into the world and, just by
chance, made himself able to do the will of God and so
on. I think you've got to think of God preparing a nation,

preparing a family, preparing a couple to have this child. I think there's planning in this from the divine side as well as the seizing of the opportunity from the human side. Yes, I think God's action is in this—in a unique way.

Reid: You and I would agree, I think, that Jesus came into the world as the result of intercourse between man and woman. Does it follow that Jesus brought with him the taint of original sin which is the lot of mankind?

Barclay: If Jesus is to be fully a man, as I believe he was, then he must come from an ordinary act of intercourse; it follows that he was not free of original sin. Now, I would like to say something about original sin because I think we need to be sure what we mean by this.

Original sin does not mean a taint of sin—that we've inherited a tendency to sin. The proper meaning of original sin in the New Testament is that we actually did sin in Adam. That you and I sinned, literally, in Adam; Adam sinned by breaking a positive commandment of God and, because he broke that commandment of God, death entered into the world. That is the Genesis story. Now, between Adam and Moses there was no law. The law didn't exist. Therefore there were no positive commandments. But, in spite of that, men continued to die. Why? Not because they had sinned themselves but because they had sinned in Adam. Original sin means that you and I are involved as persons in the sin of Adam. This is what is technically called 'solidarity'. We are 'solid' with Adam. When your nation goes to war, you go to war. You're solid with your nation. When reparations are demanded from a nation, the reparations come from the whole population. You are solid with it, and so on. The human race is solid with Adam: this is centre of Paul's doctrine.

Now, on the other hand, the human race is also solid

with Jesus Christ. It began with being solid with Adam, but since Jesus has come, we can so submit to Jesus that we can become solid with him. And, when we become solid with him, we possess his goodness just as before we possessed Adam's sin. That is New Testament theology. But as Jesus was fully a human being, as I have said, he himself must have come into the world with original sin—he too must have been solid with Adam. I would hold very strongly that Jesus could not possibly redeem that which he himself is not. In other words, what he took upon himself was fallen human nature; it was by taking fallen human nature upon himself in this way that he redeemed it.

Reid: What do you mean by 'redeem'? This is a word which we hear a lot of, but which we very often do not really understand.

Barclay: It literally means 'to buy out', 'to ransom'. But it comes to mean, in the Old Testament, 'to rescue'. For instance, when it is said that God redeemed his people from Egypt, what is meant is that he rescued them from a situation from which they could not rescue themselves. This is the basic Biblical meaning of the word 'redemption'. It ceases to be a money-transaction and comes rather to have the idea of rescue. Now it seems to me that Jesus rescues us from ourselves.

Reid: If God punishes Adam by sending death into the world, it suggests—does it not?—that God's original intention had been for Adam to live for ever.

Barclay: Indeed, and this is one of theology's problems. If Adam had not sinned, would Adam have been immortal? I don't think that the people who wrote the story ever really thought that one out.

Reid: They couldn't have, because doctors would argue

that our bodies are made in such a way that they must eventually wear out.

Barclay: Because of sin.

Reid: So illness is caused by sin? That would be the theologian's argument?

Barclay: We have to accept that there are two distinct points of view on this. The attitudes of the biologist and the theologian to sin, death and illness are diametrically opposed. On the one hand Professor Fletcher of Strathclyde University would tell you that there is nothing that religion offers that science cannot do for you. Fletcher will argue that the time will come when, if you lose an arm, they'll put a bit of new tissue on you and you will grow another arm; I think this is likely enough. But when he goes on to claim that science not only can give you peace—through tranquillisers—but also can turn the criminal into a good man, and so on; when he argues that, in another century or less, science will make us immortal, that men won't die any more (surely a dreadful thought!)—then I feel I cannot go along with him. I feel I have to revert to the theologian's approach to sin and death, which seems to me simpler and more trustworthy. Theologians express their point of view like this: *Genesis* is the book of beginnings—how did the world begin, how did sin begin, how did foreign languages begin? As for sin, it says that this began when Adam broke a positive commandment of God and once that positive commandment was broken death entered the world.

Reid: The positive commandment, I take it, was that Adam should not eat of the tree of knowledge.

Barclay: That's right.

B

Reid: Can you explain that to me?

Barclay: I don't want to explain it. This, I think, is where we
have to watch ourselves very carefully. The old, early
Bible stories are not meant to be explained. They're not
scientific, they're not philosophical, they're just
stories—with a point! Do we need to elaborate upon the
point? The point in the one we are looking at is that
Adam broke a commandment, and the commandment
was not to eat of the tree. But there's no explanation of
this. I think it's just a story.

Discussion Two

'Jesus 1'

Reid: LET'S have a closer look at Jesus. One of the problems
for the ordinary person is deciding on the nature of Jesus.
For example, how do you reconcile the two titles which
are given to him—'Son of God' and 'Son of Man'? What
do they mean to you?

Barclay: Well, in the first place, purely from the point of
view of language, Hebrew was very deficient in
adjectives. Therefore, Hebrew, instead of using an adjective, often used the phrase 'son of' plus an abstract noun.
For instance, it doesn't say that Barnabas (*Acts* 4:36)
was a consoling man, it says that Barnabas was a 'son of
consolation'. It doesn't say that James and John were
thunderous characters. It says that James and John were
'sons of thunder' (*Mark* 3:17). This is common Hebrew.
Therefore, 'Son of God' doesn't necessarily have the
same meaning as those words have in English. It need
not mean any more than God-like, in the same category
as God, in the same family as God, in the same area of
being as God. But it needn't have any idea of 'son' in the
sense that I am the son of W. D. Barclay. It hasn't beget-
ting in it, at least not in the human sense of the term.

  'Son of Man' is much more difficult to define. In
Daniel 7:13, there's a picture of four beasts—the lion,
the bear, the leopard and the ten-horned beast; these
beasts stand, with their terror, their savagery and
brutality, for the four empires which had ruled the world
up to then: the Babylonian, the Assyrian, the Persian
and the Greek. Daniel goes on, 'And then I saw one like

unto a son of man and to him was given the kingdom and
the power and the glory.' That is to say, one who was
gentle and humane—not only human but humane. This
power which was to come, in contradistinction to the
savage, beastly power of the previous kingdoms, was a
humane power. Now the Jews knew what *Daniel* 7
meant. Bit by bit they personalised '*a* son of man' until
you get, in the Authorised Version, 'like *the* son of man'.
It shouldn't be 'the'; it should be '*a* son of man'; humane.
But because they had personalised this humane figure,
'son of man' became a title of the Messiah, the person
who was to introduce the humane, gentle, loving
kingdom. Therefore, so far from being most character-
istically human, the title 'son of man' for Jesus actually
opens the way towards the superhuman because the
Messiah possessed additional superhuman qualities.

This is clearly shown in an inter-testamental book
which had a great influence upon Judaism, *The Book of
Enoch*. In it is a vision of the end, when the armies of
God are waiting to descend on the earth. The one who is
going to meet them is *that* son of man. *The Book of
Enoch*, which was probably written somewhere between
100 B.C. and A.D. 100, is almost contemporary with Jesus.
In *Enoch*, 'the son of man' has definitely become a
messianic title, without any doubt at all. I think this is
very important but it isn't taught nearly enough: 'son of
man' describes Jesus not just as a man, but as Messiah.

Reid: Of course, to be the Messiah meant that, first of all,
you were a real man, did it not? You had to be man
through and through.

Barclay: 'Messiah' is the Hebrew as 'Christ' is the Greek for
'anointed'. Three kinds of people can be anointed:
prophets, priests and kings. 'The Messiah' can describe

prophets, priests and kings. Of course, the Messiah is human all right.

Reid: Yes, this is what I thought. I thought that the fact that Jesus was called the Christ or the Messiah was testimony to his humanity.

Barclay: It is indeed—among other qualities—but I would hold that by far the best title for Jesus and the title which gets you nearest and furthest into the truth is 'the logos', 'the word', in the first chapter of John's Gospel. You see, the word 'logos' has three backgrounds.

First, in its universal background, a 'word' is two things: it's a means of communication and it's also the expression of a thought. (I want to communicate with you and I use words. I want to express my thought and I use words.) Well, if you call Jesus the word of God, Jesus is God's communication with man, and Jesus is the expression of the thought of God.

Then, in Judaism, the word is God's creative word. In Judaism, a word is not just a sound. A word *does* things. Jeremiah has it that 'the word of God breaks a rock in pieces'; the Creation story never says God made or God did: it says, 'God *said*, let there be light: and there was light.' So, secondly, the word is God's creating power. Jesus is God's recreating power; he recreates.

Thirdly we have the Greek idea of 'word' as expressed in John's Gospel. The date of John's Gospel is about A.D. 100; by that time, the Gospel was going out to the Greek world, and had to appeal to the Greek. If you talked of Jesus as the son of David to a Greek, he would have no idea who David was. So John had to find some way of speaking that would get across to Greek philosophic thought.

Heraclitus was the first person to talk about a logos—a *word*. Now Heraclitus had a central doctrine,

panta rei—everything is in a state of flux. And the
illustration that he uses again and again is this: 'Step into
a river; step out and step in again. A different river.' It
has flowed by, you see. Everything is in a state of flux.
But, although everything is in a state of flux, it is none-
theless a sensible, organised world. If you plant turnip
seeds you get turnips, not parsnips. If you put H_2O
together you'll get water, not orange juice. What does
this? What is the organising factor? The logos. According to Heraclitus and the Stoics, all things happen
according to the logos. What is the logos? The logos is
the mind of God, permeating and giving sense to the
universe, and permeating you, giving you a thinking
mind. So, if you say the word—the logos—became
flesh, what you are really saying from the Greek point of
view is that the mind of God became a human person.
That, I think, is by far the best Christology there is.

Reid: Jesus is also called 'the only son'. What does that
mean?

Barclay: It means that his sonship was unique, that Jesus is
son of God in a way that no one else is. In the fourth
Gospel, he is called THE SON, the only begotten son,
and this means that his sonship is absolutely unique. In
this case, the son of God is more than just an adjective;
it's a definition of the source of Jesus.

Reid: But I thought we had established in our first discussion that the source was Mary and Joseph?

Barclay: Oh, yes. But I don't think it's really accurate to say
that we originate only in our parents anyway. There is a
Jewish saying that, 'in the birth of any child, there are
three partners, the father and the mother and the Holy
One (blessed be he)', for the simple reason that not every
act of intercourse begets a child. This means that in any

event of conception there is God as well as the father and mother.

Reid: Are you saying, therefore, that, in the act of intercourse which produced Jesus, God was in some way more active than in the normal conception?

Barclay: This is what I would hold. It was, as so often happens, God using the normal human means for his purposes.

Reid: But does this not argue a little bit against your own suggestion that Jesus didn't come in with special advantages; you said, if he did, what good would that be to you or to me?

Barclay: Not special advantages—special purposes: just as I think for example, that God created David Livingstone to evangelise Africa. I think that God has a plan for everyone.

Reid: So we don't all have to attain to the level of Jesus?

Barclay: No. God may see a man as a good father and husband within a quite limited home; on the other hand, he sees Wilberforce as the freer of the slaves, this kind of thing.

Reid: The ordinary man is not expected, then, to arrive at a level where he is able to do the will of the Father in the way Jesus was able to do the will of the Father?

Barclay: Oh yes, he is. Very early in Christian theology, around A.D. 300, you get Christian theologians saying that the dream of God is a race of Christs. I would agree with this. I would agree that, if we do not become totally like Jesus, the fault is in our will, that we do not willingly take the same decisions that Jesus took. Looking back over your life, you are bound to see that there were things you should have done but didn't. We're all like that. It seems to me there's a lot to be said for this very old way of putting it—that the dream of God is a race of Christs.

Reid: Didn't Jesus himself indicate something of this? Didn't he say something about us all being sons of God, and that we would be able to do what he had done and maybe even more?

Barclay: He didn't bring that out particularly in the case of 'son of God'. He said, 'The things I have done you will do, and greater things also.' In John he says this.

Reid: So that doesn't support the point you were making about God's dream?

Barclay: Oh, yes! It does support it, all right. But it's a question of making the complete submission to God.

Reid: This idea of God choosing people for special purposes, great or small, has about it a suggestion of pre-destination, has it not?

Barclay: There is an epigram I once heard which has stuck to me all through my teaching life. 'Fate is what we *must* do. Destiny is what we are meant to do.' I think that every man has a destiny, but no man has a fate.

Reid: Did Jesus claim to be God at any time?

Barclay: I can't think of any incident. You can quote things like, 'I and my Father are one', but then you can turn round and quote the other thing, 'my Father is greater than I.' You see, what I think is wrong here is this: we are thinking of the connection of Jesus with God in the wrong terms. Jesus said of Christians, 'I pray that they may be one as we are one.' Now, he prays that Christians may be one with each other as he is one with God. But what is the oneness of Christianity? The oneness of Christianity is, 'By this shall all men know that you are my disciples, that you have love one for another.' The oneness of Christianity is love. Therefore, the oneness of Jesus with God is love. We are not to think in terms of philosophy and essences and all that kind of thing. We are to think in terms of personal relationships. The personal relationship of God with Jesus is a love that is perfect. And what is the sign of a perfect love? The sign of a perfect love is perfect obedience.

Reid: How then do you think that Jesus acquired this perfect obedience to God?

Barclay: I don't know. There's this empty period in Jesus' life. We know nothing about him between his birth and the age of thirty, except for the one appearance in the temple when he was a boy of twelve. But I can't help feeling that his parents must have had something to do with it. I've often felt that we don't give Joseph enough prominence in the life of Jesus. If Jesus thought of God basically and above all as Father, the content of the word 'father' must have come from Joseph.

Reid: What do you mean by the content of the word 'father'?

Barclay: Well, he must have learned what fatherhood means from Joseph. Luther could never bear to pray 'Our Father' because his father had been so stern with him. The word 'father' painted a picture which frightened him. But one thing that we can truly say of Jesus is that the word 'father' didn't paint a picture that frightened him. It painted a picture which was perfect. The content of this picture must surely have come from Joseph.

Reid: Do you feel then that Jesus must have undergone a period of spiritual training of some kind?

Barclay: It says so. In Luke we are told that 'Jesus grew in
wisdom and in stature and in favour with God and man.'
He grew in wisdom; he grew in favour with God and
man. If there was no growth in the life of Jesus, then he
was not a man at all. You can't possibly imagine the
baby at Mary's breast saying, 'I am the son of God.' This
is something that Jesus had to learn, and he had to learn
it at home as much as anywhere else.

Reid: Do you think that he developed his great awareness of
God through his everyday living with people, with men
and women? Or did he acquire it in some more esoteric
way?

Barclay: I think it must have been both ways because, when
he went out on the roads of Palestine on his mission, one
of the things we notice is that, again and again, he goes
off to be alone, and I don't reckon that this is something
which he only did when he started to go out on the roads
of Palestine. I reckon these periods of aloneness were
part of his life all the time, even in Nazareth. And I think
he saw God in people. He must have seen God in the synagogue because obviously he was a regular attender. He
saw God in scripture because he could quote scripture,
as he did, for instance, in his temptations. And I think he
saw God directly in the times when he was alone.
Another way we can put it is that he saw God in prayer.

Reid: What would the act of prayer entail with Jesus?
Would it be saying words to God or would it be just
sitting quietly?

Barclay: I think that the prayers we hear Jesus praying
mostly are prayers 'that your will be done'. They are
prayers in which he speaks of submitting himself to the
will of God. I think that Jesus must always have asked
for the help that he wanted, but that he concluded every

prayer with the words, 'your will be done'. That was where the obedience came from. He was the one person who had learned to make all prayer, 'your will be done.'

Reid: Why is this so hard for the rest of us, and for people all down the ages?

Barclay: Because in regard to prayer nearly all of us constitutionally pray, 'your will be changed.'

Reid: What is it in us that makes us like this? Is it some force of evil?

Barclay: If you like, you can call it that; but it is the putting of self into the centre of the picture. Surely what makes us take this way is that, instead of making God the most important person in life, we put ourselves and our wants in the centre of the picture. In other words, all sin comes from the magnification of self.

Reid: I think it was Paul Tillich who described sin as our 'estrangement from God' and, to me, that seems to be a very acceptable and helpful definition. What would you say about that?

Barclay: I would say that, for the ordinary man, it must be pretty-well meaningless. I mean, 'estrangement from God'—the ordinary man's not worried! You need to give him something much more definite than that.

Reid: It's hard to be more definite. But I suppose that Tillich means that man is no longer trying in any way to do God's will, only trying to do his own will, and this is sin.

Barclay: If he puts it that way, that's a bit different, isn't it? I mean, it sounds different. But what the ordinary man, the common man, will come back at you with is, 'how can I know God's will?'

Reid: Well, how do you know God's will? That is the big question.

Barclay: There are a lot of ways in which I know God's will. In the first instance, quite simply, there is the matter of conscience. Our consciences are pretty active. In the second instance, there is the matter of the Bible. In the third instance, there is the church. You get it there. In the fourth instance, there are good people whom we trust. We get it there. And, fifthly, we get it directly from the Holy Spirit.

Reid: I find it hard to believe that you can find out God's will in the first four of these ways. You can find out, perhaps, what men think God's will is, or what the church thinks God's will is, but that's not quite the same, is it?

Barclay: My answer to that would be something that is quite unhelpful but which I am bound to say is true, and that is that I've never ever, literally never once, had any doubt about God's will. Time and time again, I haven't done it, but I've never been ignorant of what it was.

Reid: I would think that you are pretty unique in that.

Barclay: I don't think so. I think I am merely honest. An awful lot of people just don't want to know God's will. They say they don't know it when they know it fine.

Reid: Can you give me an example of when you really knew that something was God's will?

Barclay: I would think almost everything, any particular thing I've ever done.

Reid: Well, let us consider this book we are working on at the moment. Would you say that this is God's will?

Barclay: In this particular case, the writing of a book, I regard it as a professional job, and I wouldn't ask so much if it is God's will. But I would expect to get evidence, if it wasn't God's will, that I shouldn't do it.

Reid: Well, this is what was in my mind earlier on when you gave me your five ways of discerning God's will. The first four seemed to me, at best, to be negative ways of finding out God's will. They would give us the answer to the things we shouldn't do. But they wouldn't so easily indicate those things which we ought to do. For example, if I were an employer of men and I wanted to get rid of an old faithful servant who was no longer much use to me, I can see that my conscience, the church, the Bible and good people would all probably try to restrain me. They might convince me that the action I wanted to take was not God's will. But it seems much harder to get from these four agencies, in any given situation, a positive answer to what God's will may be.

Barclay: I don't know. The Stoics used to talk a great deal about God's will. They had a phrase, 'arresting ideas'. The word used for arresting was precisely the same word used by a policeman putting his hand on your shoulder and saying, 'I arrest you.' Now I would think that the ideas of right and wrong are like that. You won't normally get reasons for them at all. You will just know that this is the right thing, or this is the wrong thing to do.

Reid: Do you feel that God speaks in a whisper—'the still small voice?' This is my feeling. I feel that he doesn't shout at us. He gives very quiet indications which we can mishear or avoid hearing very easily.

Barclay: I think this is true, except that sometimes you get an overwhelming conviction that you must do something. But, on the whole, I think I agree with you. I certainly agree that he doesn't shout at us. This is a good way of putting it. I mean, there's a certain politeness about God. He doesn't force himself on your attentions.

Reid: But, of course, he could, couldn't he? I wonder why he doesn't?

Barclay: Because there is no value in anything that is not given of your free will.

Reid: Is there free will? Aren't we conditioned all the time by the people and the events which make up our lives?

Barclay: We are conditioned all the time. This is perfectly true. We are not, however, at the mercy of our conditions. We can always break them. I agree that this is the problem of society and the problem of civilisation, that we are conditioned by our environment and by our heredity, and all this kind of thing. We are not, as I have suggested, absolutely bound by these things. They do make life very much more difficult for some people than for others. I always remember a sermon by Fosdick entitled, 'No man need stay the way he is,' and this, I think, is profoundly true. No man need stay the way he is.

Reid: And yet, for all of us, it's very hard to change, isn't it? We rather like the way we are, don't we?

Barclay: Yes, that's absolutely true. You won't be changed, you have to change.

Reid: And this is difficult.

Barclay: Yes, we're fairly well pleased with ourselves. I quite agree with that.

'Jesus 2'

Reid: WHAT were the most important factors in Jesus' life? Were they the things that he said, or the things that he did, or neither?

Barclay: I don't think that you can separate what he did and what he said. Time and time again, what he said emerged directly out of what he was doing. Many, many, many of his sermons, his discussions, proceeded directly from some miracle he had done. The theological answer to your question would be that neither of these things was the most important. The most important thing was not what Jesus said or did, but what Jesus was. His deeds and words were so united in his life that you can't say his deeds were the most important, you can't say his words were the most important. There was an interlocking between deed and word which is precisely where so many of us go wrong: our words and our deeds don't interlock.

Reid: One of the hard things which Jesus said was to let the dead bury the dead. To many people, this seems a very cruel thing to say.

Barclay: Yes, he said to the man, 'Follow me' and the man said, 'Let me first go and bury my father.' But you see, this was a common saying in Palestine. What the man meant was 'I'll come with you when my father dies', not that his father was dead. His father may have been about forty. This is what the man really meant: 'I'll come with you in 25 years' time when my father dies.' So Jesus' reply was not cruel. He was simply saying, 'Make up your mind.' Somebody may challenge me to go to the mission field and I'll say, 'I'll go when I've buried my wife.' In other words, I'll go when my wife dies.

Reid: So the man was really putting off?

Barclay: He was dodging the issue with a vengeance. So often our failure to understand the New Testament or our failure to accept it comes from our failure to understand some kind of local custom or local way of speaking that was common in the time of Jesus.

Reid: One of the things that Christians claim to be unique in their religion is the emphasis upon loving your neighbour. I once, however, heard a Jew on the wireless claim that this commandment occurs in one of the books of the Old Testament, *Leviticus*.

Barclay: In *Leviticus* your neighbour is your fellow Jew and you must love him. But it didn't say that you must love everyone, Jew and non-Jew alike.

Reid: So this is the big difference?

Barclay: Yes, and the other big difference is that you must do to others as you would have them do to you. This is hardly ever, if ever, found anywhere else in a positive form. It's quite often said, in fact in most moralities it is said, that you must not do to others what you would not like them to do to you, which is easy compared with doing to others, in the positive form, what you would want them to do to you. It's quite easy not to do the wrong thing but, to go out of your way to do the good thing is quite a different thing altogether. This is at least part of the Christian originality.

Reid: Jesus certainly didn't receive much of this positive goodness which he preached. Not only did they fail to do

to him the things they would like to have done for themselves, they did that thing which they themselves would
not want to have done to themselves. They killed him.
Many people do not understand why it was that Jesus
had to die on the cross in order to save us.

Barclay: Well, let us go back to what we said on an earlier
occasion about Jesus being the word, that Jesus is the
complete expression of the mind of God. (See p. 13.) In
Jesus, the mind of God became a person. Now
according to Jesus, God is love. Therefore, Jesus came
into this world to say to men, 'God loves you.' He came
in to say to them, 'God loves you no matter what you do
to him.' He came in to say, 'I love you no matter what
you do to me.' They hated him, they were traitors to him,
they opposed him, they stood up against him, they tried
him, and all the time he was saying to them, 'No matter
what you do, I still love you.' If he had stopped anywhere
before death, it would have meant that, at some point he
said, 'Thus far and no further. My love stops here.' But
he says, by going to the cross, 'You can reject me, you
can scourge me, you can revile me, you can crucify me.
You will not stop me loving you.' That is why he had to
die, in my view. I don't think that the death of Christ had
anything to do with a sacrifice for the forgiveness of sins.

Reid: This is the question I wanted to get on to. I have never
been happy with this idea of sacrifice.

Barclay: I think what Jesus came to do was to demonstrate
what God is like. You see, if you say that the death of
Jesus was a sacrifice to save men from their sins, what
you are really saying is that by dying he made God
change his mind, that up to that moment God was going
to bash us and, after that moment, God said, 'I'll hold my
hand because this man died.' Now, if this is true, it means
that God was compelled to change his mind by Jesus,

and it means something worse. It means that, to satisfy
the demands of his justice, God was guilty of the greatest
injustice anybody has ever been guilty of: he punished
the only good man who ever lived. So I don't think this
sense of sacrifice as a payment for our sins enters into it
at all. Jesus' death is to show us that nothing, nothing we
do, can stop him loving us.

Now, there's another word, 'cost', which we can put in
place of the word 'sacrifice'. It cost the death of Jesus to
demonstrate the absolute limitless love of God.

Reid: Therefore, the culmination of all that Jesus was and
is, was in his sentence, 'Father, forgive them'?

Barclay: Yes, if you like.

Reid: That was the pinnacle of it? It had all led up to his
being able to say that on the cross? That, you say,
demonstrated his love for everyone, and God's love?

Barclay: It demonstrated Jesus' love but, because it does
that, it also demonstrates God's love; whatever Jesus is
doing is what God is doing.

Reid: If Jesus hadn't said these words, if he had just died on
the cross, would it not have made a difference?

Barclay: No, I don't think so. They weren't the last things
he said by any means. I think it was just that he would go
to death when, quite easily, he could have caused a re-
bellion and got away with it. But he chose, quite
deliberately, to say, 'You can do what you like with me.
It doesn't stop me loving you.'

Reid: How does he show that it doesn't stop him loving
them? How does this come through?

Barclay: It comes through in his words, 'Father, forgive
them.' But there's more than that. You see, we're in the

position of being able to read the story of Jesus from beginning to end, knowing the end. We're not like the people in the middle of it. Now Jesus' love comes through in the fact that he refused to be turned into an armed revolutionary. *John*, chapter six, tells how they came and tried to make him a king, but he slipped out of their hands and away he went. He would not be turned into someone who uses force. Rather than use force, he would go to the cross.

Reid: There have been other martyrs. What was unique about Jesus' going to the cross for his convictions?

Barclay: What was unique was that he so definitely didn't need to do it.

Reid: You feel that he could have avoided the cross?

Barclay: I don't feel it. It's obvious. He needn't have gone to Jerusalem. He could have gone back to Galilee where he would have been absolutely safe. He would then have been out of the jurisdiction of the Jerusalem government.

Reid: Is it evident that, when he went into Jerusalem, he was aware of what awaited him?

Barclay: Absolutely. He said so over and over again. He started just after Peter's confession at Caesarea Philippi by saying, 'The Son of man goes to Jerusalem where they will take him and crucify him and, after three days, he will rise again.' From that time forward, he never stops telling them that he's going to die.

Reid: Of course, another reason for the Crucifixion would be to enable the Resurrection to take place because you couldn't have the Resurrection without the Crucifixion.

Barclay: The whole meaning of the Resurrection, whatever happened, is the liberation of Jesus. In John Masefield's play *Good Friday*, Procula, Pilate's wife who was supposed not to want the Crucifixion to take place, is talking with Longinas, the centurion in charge of the Crucifixion. Longinas says, 'He was a fine, young fellow but, when we were finished with him, he was a poor, broken thing on a cross.' Procula says, 'So, you think he's dead and gone forever?' Then Longinas says, 'No, madam, I do not. He is set free throughout the world where neither Jew nor Greek can stop his truth.' This is what the resurrection did for Jesus. It liberated him from being able to be only in one place at one time—from being able to speak to only a limited number of people.

Reid: I can follow that up to a point. But how then was Jesus able to communicate to the wider audience after he was resurrected?

Barclay: The answer is that this is something which, as Christians, we should know happens. I mean, everyone who has any claim to be a Christian must at some time have been aware either of the presence of his Lord without any words at all or of the words of Jesus.

Reid: Let us say that Jesus had just died in the normal way. People would still have told us about this marvellous man who went about doing good, who did miracles and who loved everyone. What would have been missing?

Barclay: The Resurrection. Without it, there would have been no church.

Reid: No church without the Resurrection?

Barclay: You can't have a church which worships a dead man.

Reid: So you feel that the church worships Jesus, not God?

Barclay: The church is aware of the living Christ, or should be.

Reid: Living in the sense that he overcame death, and people could testify that he overcame death. That's what is meant by the living Christ?

Barclay: Yes, but we've got two things. We've got the Resurrection which, according to the New Testament, lasted for forty days. Then we've got the living Christ who lasts for ever and ever. Now I think we've got to be very careful about this resurrection business. I think that, without any possible doubt, there was a subjective element about the Resurrection. You will note, if you read the New Testament, that Jesus never appeared to anyone except those who loved him, and people who were talking about him on the road to Emmaus. I think this is the key to the New Testament doctrine of the Resurrection; that Jesus never appeared except to people who loved him. And I think that two people could have been in a room together, one who loved Jesus and one who was quite indifferent, and one would have seen him and the other wouldn't.

Reid: Does the Bible give us real reason for believing that the Risen Christ was a reality?

Barclay: I think the Bible's definite about this. But I don't think the Bible's the only proof of it. I think the proof of this is that, when Jesus was crucified, the disciples all forsook him and fled. Apparently, they just decided that they would go back to fishing. Something has to be assumed to have happened to explain the alteration from being eleven terrified men to being, seven weeks later, men who were prepared to defy the mob and defy the Sanhedrin by saying that, 'We do what God thinks right'. The only thing that can reasonably explain this is the conviction that Jesus was risen from the dead.

Discussion Four

'The Bible'

Reid: I WAS once very impressed by a preacher who said that the Bible is not the word of God, that it only becomes the word of God when the things that the Bible says are put into practice by human beings. Would you go along with that?

Barclay: I don't think so. I think what he said implies much too great a quantity of subjectivity. I don't think the Bible is the word of God in the sense that it's a *verbatim* transcript of what God said. On the contrary I think that God speaks, not in words but in events: and the Bible is the record of God's actions and events throughout the centuries and throughout the years, written by men as they saw it. I would think that the two most important things to remember about the Bible are quite simple.

First, the Bible is not a book. It is a very considerable collection of books. This collection of books took a long, long time to write and a still longer time to make; I suppose that the earliest book in the Old Testament was *The Book of Amos* which was written about 850 B.C. while the last book to be written was probably *Daniel*, about 170 B.C. The Old Testament took 700 years to write but the timescale of events in it was a lot longer because the children of Israel left Egypt in the Exodus about 1,400 B.C., and Abraham was five hundred years before that. So you could say that you have got 2,000 years of events taking 700 years to write. Then you come to the New Testament; the earliest book in the New Testament is probably the *Letter to the Galatians*, somewhere about A.D. 48–49 and the latest *The Second Letter of Peter*, say about A.D. 120. So again you have about 80 years in the writing and if you add 120 to 850 B.C., the Bible took a thousand years to write. The first time the Old Testament achieved its present form was at the Council of Jamnia in A.D. 90. (This was a council of rabbis who settled the books of the Old Testament.) And the first occasion the New Testament is set out with the books we know in it, is in the *Letter of Athanasius*, whose date is A.D. 346. The whole Bible consists of books which are there because they wouldn't die, because people insisted upon using them.

Secondly, you can't expect a man to have the same ideas of science and the world in 850 B.C. as he has today. He didn't know what the world was like. For him, the earth would be the centre of the universe, not the sun. You have to remember when you read the Bible that it was written by men whose science and whose knowledge of the world were primitive, and were certainly not ours. It is right, similarly, to say not that the Bible is the word of God but that the Bible contains the word of God. I think this is an important point to get: the Bible is a record of man's developing grasp of revelation. He can be told only as much as he can understand: he grasps revelation bit by bit. I should hope we are still grasping revelation piecemeal as time goes by.

Reid: If you say that the Bible is not the word of God but that it contains the word of God, are you saying therefore that some parts are far more important than other parts?

Barclay: Oh, unquestionably. There are vast sections of the Bible that no Christian believes are binding for himself, such as the food-laws and the sacrificial laws. I mean, we are told in the Bible that we mustn't eat pork. It doesn't stop you ordering a pork chop in a restaurant or having bacon and egg for your breakfast. When a woman had a baby in Palestine, she was unclean for forty days if it was a boy, and eighty if it was a girl. At the end of it she went to the Temple and offered a pigeon and a ram for her cleansing. Well, you don't think of your wife as being unclean for forty or eighty days or in need of ritual purification after a birth, or that kind of thing! There are all kinds of things mentioned in the Old Testament which were only local and temporary; the point about these is that they were not unimportant in their day. The laws about food and about cleansing and sacrifices were what made the Jew different from other people. The Jew is not now a different physical type from other people. What makes him different is his religion. My daughter Jane had a very close friend, a little Jewish girl of her own age. When they were about six or seven, we would take Diane out with us for a run in the car on a Saturday afternoon and we would stop at some hotel for afternoon tea and the sandwiches would arrive. The first thing Diane would say was, 'Mr Barclay, can I eat them?' And, of course, if they were ham, she couldn't eat them. But I used to think it was magnificent that a child of seven should, in a public restaurant or hotel, witness to her faith. This is what made a Jew. The food-laws separate the Jews. They are a holy people. Now the word 'holy' in the Bible always means 'different' or 'separate': 'remember the Sabbath day to keep it holy'; to keep it different from other days. The Jewish people are holy—they are different from other people and the difference was observed in these food-laws and sacrificial laws and so forth. So they were not a waste of time; they are a layer in the building and not the final building.

Again, a very considerable part of the Old Testament was about animal sacrifice; you offer this, that and the next sacrifice to God. But we nowadays don't sacrifice an animal to God at all. Are we then to say that this is quite irrelevant? No! When these things were written, the most expensive and most valuable things that a man had was his farm stock and, if you offered your animal to God, you were offering your most precious possession to God. So what sacrifice basically means is, 'I will take my dearest possession and offer it to God'; under Christianity, that, of course, is one's self.

The other thing which is probably used against the Old Testament more than anything else, is what people call the blood-thirsty character of the Old Testament: you killed every man, woman and child in a captured city. The Jew, in fact, was desperately afraid of his religion becoming in any way infected; to avoid infection, he simply wiped out his enemies. Of course, we would think the way to wipe out the enemies of Christ would be to convert them, but what the Jew is doing when he says, in the old days, 'Wipe them all out', is trying desperately to preserve the cleanness, the purity of his religion. Underlying this there's the great truth that you have got to make men believers and not unbelievers. Blood-thirst and sacrifice, on the face of it, are out of date, but underneath lies a principle which is still just as powerful as ever. Now this is true of a great deal of the Bible. You've got to get at the principle which lies beneath to discover the binding thing for us.

Reid: For the modern Christian, then, would it be any disadvantage if he just disregarded the Old Testament?

Barclay: Well, the loss would be this. You don't understand a child until you know something of the home he was brought up in and the home which he came from. You don't understand Christianity until you understand something of the cradle of Judaism from which it came.

Historically, it would be disastrous to ditch the Old Testament, and I think that religiously it would, too. I mean, you can say what you like, but you can't get any morality which is not really founded in the Ten Commandments. You can't get any morality, as opposed to liturgy and all this kind of thing, any greater than you get amongst the prophets who insisted that you could have the finest services in the world but if you don't love your fellow man, the whole thing is useless. And you have got this in the Old Testament. But what I think is true to say is that none of the Bible is intelligible, really, without a commentary. The Bible is like everything else which is 2,000 years old. It needs the expert to interpret it. Not so much to argue about it, but simply to tell you what it is all about, what it means, how it came to be written and I think much, much more of this needs to be done.

Reid: This seems to lead us into another path whereby you almost seem to be suggesting that, in order to know about God and perhaps in order to lead the good life, a certain level of intellectual ability, either in yourself or in somebody else, is necessary—that God can only work through the intellect.

Barclay: No, I would suggest that the simplest person can *appropriate* Christianity, and the help that Christianity and religion can give. The simplest person can enjoy it, the simplest person can use it. But, for the *propagation* and communication of Christianity, you need an intelligent approach to it, too. I think the simplest analogy is that anyone can go into a garden and appreciate the beauty and perfume of the flowers but if you want to grow and develop them, you need to know some botany—you need some expert knowledge. And I think this is true of Christianity. Anybody can appropriate it, but if you are going to explain, propagate and preach it, I think you need some expert knowledge as well.

May I use an illustration I've often used in this? I only once heard Tillich lecture. Now Tillich, as everyone knows, could be extremely obscure and in this lecture he was obscure. When he had finished, there was a burst of applause from a lot of people who I am quite sure didn't understand a word, but who at least thought something fine was going on. I had tea afterwards with Tillich and a group of University teachers. I was young then and cheeky. I probably wouldn't have done it now. I said to him, 'Professor Tillich, did you expect anyone to understand a word of what you were talking about this afternoon?' He said, 'Oh, no.' So I said then, 'This means that you are starting a new kind of gnosticism, that Christianity is for the intellectually élite and that simple persons like myself are simply just not there.' He said, 'Oh, no.' So I said, 'Well, you'll need to explain, because your two "Oh no's" don't seem to add up!' So he said, 'Well, it's as simple as this. Anyone can grasp religion. A child can grasp religion. What is difficult is the conceptualisation of religion.' Now, what he meant was, anybody can grasp the effect, the power, the strength of religion, but the difficulty comes when you try to put this matter into a coherent system that you can transmit to someone else. So, if you like, you can say it is the difference between religion and theology.

Reid: Talking of Tillich, and still remaining on the subject of the Bible, he once said that he thought that certain forms of fundamentalism are a soul-destroying demonization of Christianity because they foster dishonesty. What would you say about that?

Barclay: I have great sympathy with the fundamentalists. What a fundamentalist feels is that you must accept all or nothing; that if you cast doubts on one part of the

Bible, then you have lost faith in it all. Actually, I am not quite sure about this, but I believe that the fundamentals from which the name 'fundamentalist' comes, derive from a series of tracts which were printed in the late 19th century in America which were called *The Fundamentals of the Christian Religion*; one was on the substitutionary atonement, another was on the physical resurrection of Jesus Christ, and another was on the physical second coming. You see the kind of thing. They are all very literal, very physical things. There were five of them. I have forgotten what the other two were.

Reid: Was virgin birth one of them?

Barclay: Virgin birth was one. That is correct. Now, what I have felt all along is that you actually lose a lot if you insist on being literal. I think the best example of this is unquestionably the Jonah story. If you insist on taking the story of Jonah literally, you've got the story of a man swallowed by a big fish. Not a whale—it's a big fish. And he's vomited up again and that's that. But if you take the story of Jonah symbolically, if you interpret it symbolically, you get Jonah as being by far the greatest book in the Old Testament.

Remember the story. The story is that Jonah was sent to Nineveh which is on the east of the Mediterranean, and he promptly ran away to Tarshish which is in Spain, as far away as he could possibly get. But on the way there was a storm. He was flung out—he was swallowed by the fish and he had to go to Nineveh and there he preached. To his intense disgust, the people repented and he went out and sat and waited for the people to be destroyed, and they weren't destroyed. Now God had caused a plant to give him shelter and the plant perished in the night and Jonah was very annoyed. And God said to Jonah, 'Are you terribly annoyed about this plant

—yet you don't care tuppence about hundreds of thousands of people, animals, children and women who are going to be wiped out?' Now the point is that 'Jonah' is the nation of Israel. Israel was meant to take God's truth to men and God's love to men and wouldn't. Israel became the most exclusive nation instead of the most missionary nation. Israel was swallowed by the exile. The fish is the exile, and the exile yanked them out of Palestine whether they wanted it or not. They got a chance to preach, and still they would rather see people damned to hell than converted because they wanted to keep God to themselves. And it is that which Jonah is up against, which is tremendous and marvellous. This is the only missionary book in the Old Testament, the only missionary Judaistic book there is.

That's where I think the fundamentalist loses. I don't think he's dishonest. I think he's afraid. He's like a man who's hanging on by his fingertips refusing to let go when his feet are only six inches from the ground. You see, what the fundamentalist really wants is authority. He wants to be able to say, 'The Bible says . . .' Now what he really is afraid of is freedom.

Reid: This is interesting to me because the thing that I find irritating about those people whom I class as fundamentalists is this very thing you have mentioned. Whenever there is a discussion or an argument, it is 'the Bible says this', or 'the Bible says that'. It seems to me to be the only way they can talk.

Barclay: Of course! The answer to that is that you can always quote an equal and opposite text. This is where you do find that fundamentalism, so to speak, signs its own death-warrant. Because, if you quote a text on one side, you can quote a text on the other. A famous one that we have already quoted in our talks is that Jesus said, 'I and my Father are one'. But Jesus also said, 'My Father is greater than I'. And again, you may talk about the Virgin Birth, but on more than one occasion, Jesus was called 'the son of Joseph' in the New Testament.

Fundamentalism doesn't really give you this security which people want so much. This, of course, is also the power of the Roman Catholic Church. The fundamentalists have an infallible book. The Catholics have an infallible church. Both can say, 'the Bible says' or 'the church says', and that finishes all argument, which is comfortable, I suppose. When I was a student, there was a progression of a number of famous people to the Catholic church. To take three, there was Hilaire Belloc, there was G. K. Chesterton and there was John Swinerton Phillimore, who taught me Latin, and I am sure they all gravitated to the Roman church because they were tired of the arguments and the doubts and the debates of the Protestant Church.

Reid: What do you think about people who, when they have a problem, take down the Bible and open it at random in the hope of finding the answer to their problem?

Barclay: I think it is pretty well mad. There is a very interesting story about that. A man who wanted advice opened the Bible, and the first thing he read was that Judas went out and hanged himself. This didn't seem very helpful advice. He tried again; lo and behold, the first text his eye fell on was 'go thou and do likewise'. So he tried for a third time and the book fell open and he looked again and it said, 'what thou doest, do quickly'! You laugh, but it is quite as sensible as many of the bits of advice you would get from the Bible. I don't think that one's attitude to any problem, any action or any belief should be settled by any single text or any single biblical incident. What one has to do is to take the whole of the

Bible to every situation. For instance, you apply the love of God to a situation. I mean, you would not take the story of Sodom and Gomorrah as being the only thing God is. You would apply the whole of God, and the whole of God is, in the end, love, to the particular situation concerning you.

Reid: What is a good way for the average layman to make use of his Bible, to get the best out of it? I know you have said he should have a commentary.

Barclay: Oh yes, he must have a commentary to get the best out of everything. He must, in the first instance, have a modern translation.

Reid: Such as?

Barclay: Well, *The New English Bible* or, I think, sometimes even better, *The Jerusalem Bible*. One of the two. He must, in the first instance, have a modern translation. You see, the Old Testament was written in classical Hebrew, in beautiful Hebrew, but the New Testament is written in the colloquial Greek which people spoke in the street. In fact, it is the only literary monument of that colloquial Greek. The New Testament Greek is not far off the English of *The Daily Express*. It is the kind of thing which is spoken in the street between ordinary people, and therefore any archaic translation is a bad translation. The 'thous' and 'thees' are the kind of thing which shouldn't be there. So, first of all, he needs a new translation, but even when he gets a new translation there will still be a lot of things he needs help with. For example, no new translation will tell him what a Pharisee or a Sadducee is. He'll need to get a commentary in order to find this out. And he'll not get any idea, for instance, of what Palestine is. I mean, Palestine is only one hundred and seventy miles from north to south and it is only forty two miles from east to west. This is to say it is further from Edinburgh to Glasgow or from London to Brighton than it is across the whole of Palestine. Unless he gets a book which will tell him some of these facts, he can never picture the way things happened in Palestine. So he needs a modern translation and he needs a commentary and, I think I would really have to say, he needs a group. I don't think any man will get the best out of the Bible reading it alone.

Reid: Why not?

Barclay: Because he will interpret it to suit himself. Jerome translated *The Vulgate*, the Catholic Bible. Jerome translated it alone, and Luther said he lost the promise that, 'where two or three are gathered together, there am I in the midst of them'. I wouldn't like to interpret a Greek secular text alone, for I know I would read all my own prejudices into it. He needs the combined experience, and the combined wisdom of a group. Not a big group. A group small enough to study and small enough to talk intimately to each other.

Reid: We spoke earlier on about the Roman Catholic Bible. Am I right in thinking that the books of the Apocrypha are included in their Bible? If so, why did these apocryphal books get into the Roman Catholic Bible if they were not considered good enough for the Protestant Bible?

Barclay: The Roman Catholic Bible came originally from *The Vulgate*, and *The Vulgate* is Latin, and the Latin translations were not made originally from the Hebrew direct; nobody knew Hebrew because it had got practically lost. They were made from *The Septuagint*, the Greek translation of the Old Testament which was begun about 270 B.C. It was made in Alexandria, and

Alexandria allowed quite a lot of extra books into the Greek version and, when the Council of Jamnia to which I have already referred (See p. 31) listed the books of the Old Testament, the first principle of the listing was that no book would get in which was not originally written in Hebrew. Now this is to say the Hebrew Bible contains only the books written in Hebrew and that is what the English Bible contains too. But because *The Vulgate* came *via* the Greek it included certain other books and these books were *The Apocrypha*. The word 'Apocrypha' means books which were not to be read at public worship but which were to be read secretly by oneself. I think I would now cheerfully put in at least two of these books.

Reid: Which ones?

Barclay: Ecclesiasticus and *Wisdom. Ecclesiasticus* might well have got in because it was written originally in Hebrew but the Hebrew had been lost and has only been re-discovered in our own time.

Reid: Are the other ones of no great value then?

Barclay: Oh no, there are at least two of them which are of inestimable value. *First* and *Second Maccabees*, because they have got the history of the Jewish wars and the collapse of Jerusalem among other things. They are good history. Some of them, like *Tobias and the Angel*, are wonderful stories and some are great poetry. On the whole, whilst you can easily feel the difference between them and the real thing of the Old Testament, I think it is a great pity that they ever got so completely lost as they have in the Protestant Church. There are three views of *The Apocrypha*. To the Roman Catholic church they are scripture; to the Church of England they are not scripture but can be read openly in public worship. To the

c

Presbyterian church they are anathema from the beginning.

Reid: What exactly do we mean by 'scripture'?

Barclay: Well, this is a very difficult question; I would say that, from the practical point of view, scripture consists of these books which, throughout the ages, the Church has come to regard as final and authoritative. But, when a man wrote a book which ultimately got into the Bible, he certainly did not sit down and say, 'I'm going to write a book of scripture.' It survived, as I have already said, simply because it helped people. It's the survival of the fittest which explains the whole rise of the Bible.

Reid: The word 'scripture' raises another question in my mind, and that is the things that happen in the New Testament so that scripture might be fulfilled. I always have my doubts about these things. I am a bit sceptical.

Barclay: The phrases, 'This was done that scripture might be fulfilled' and 'this happened that scripture might be fulfilled', come mainly in *Matthew*. This was a Gospel written by a Jew for Jews, and the one way he could present Jesus was to present him as the fulfilment of Jewish hopes, prophecies and dreams. But he does it in a way that no modern man could do at all. I take only one example. He explains the journey into Egypt of the holy family by a prophecy from Hosea which says, 'Out of Egypt have I called my son'. But the Hosea prophecy has nothing to do with Jesus. It is the statement of how God called the children of Israel from their slavery out of Egypt. It just reads, 'Out of Israel have I called my son'. Matthew grabs this as it is exactly what he wants.

Reid: So there is a sort of cheating quality about this writing then?

Barclay: No, this is the step that you mustn't take. It wasn't cheating in A.D. 50 or 60. It was accepted exegesis. I think it is cheating now when you know better. But it wasn't cheating to do it in A.D. 50 or 60. It was the then accepted means of exegesis. If you want to speak about cheating, I would suppose that the most gorgeously beautiful book of the Old Testament is *The Song of Solomon.* I don't myself have any doubt that *The Song of Solomon* is just a magnificent series of love songs, an anthology of love songs, and that the love it's talking about is physical love. But the exegetes very early on allegorised this into the love of God for his people, or the love of Christ for his church. It is not cheating. It is certainly reading into the book meanings that were not originally there; but, this was the standard and accepted form of exegesis. It may indicate a certain ignorance of the facts of the case; it may indicate, for instance, a certain prejudice against physical love; but it is not cheating—for that is how it was done in those days.

Reid: Isn't there quite a lot of scholarly evidence to suggest that much of the Bible, including the New Testament, has been 'written up'?

Barclay: I don't see how you can help writing up a thing when you know the end of the story before you begin. You see, this is the point. Those who wrote the New Testament weren't writing from page to page without knowing what came next. They knew the whole story before they started and, because of this, certain things, certain happenings in Jesus' life, obviously had a significance that they wouldn't otherwise have seen. Therefore, there is a certain writing up. I mean, what you can quite legitimately say is that the Gospels in particular were written by men who already believed that Jesus Christ was the Son of God, our Saviour. In that belief they tend to see all that he was, said, and did. The other way to put it is the way the theologians would put it, that all the Gospels are *post*-resurrection narratives. They are all written in the light and the awareness that Jesus was more than the carpenter of Nazareth—that he was, and is, in fact, the risen Christ.

'The Church'

Reid: You and I are both members of the church, and I
think you would agree that the Church is not the most
potent force today. What can be done about it?

Barclay: I think we have got to go back and see how the
whole business started. The Greek for church is *ekklesia.*
An *ekklesia* literally means a picked-out assembly. This
term came from Athens, and when Athens was at its
biggest, its best and its greatest, its total population
wasn't much more than 26,000, extraordinary to say.
But every single male citizen who had a certain amount
of money was a member of the *ekklesia*—the ruling
body. What happened was that when the *ekklesia* was
due to meet, the herald went through the streets and said,
'The *ekklesia* is meeting at such and such a time, at such
and such a place. Come.' The *ekklesia* in fact consisted,
not of everyone, but of those who accepted the invitation.

If you go back to the early church, bearing in mind
this idea of accepting an invitation, I think you get a very
clear idea of what the church was. It was over 200 years
before the church had any buildings; being illegal, they
simply couldn't build them. So most of the preaching
was done on the street. What must have happened over
and over again would be this: a man would be going
down the street and he would come across a Christian
preacher at the street corner. The heathen man might
stop to listen. If he was very interested, he might stop to
listen right through; at the end, he might go up to the

preacher or to the person who was keeping order, and he
might say to them, 'Tell me, where can I find out more
about this Jesus?' He would then be directed to one of
the Christian gatherings which met in houses. So his
object in coming to church was, 'Where can I find out
more about Jesus?' He didn't come because he felt he
was perfect. He didn't come because he felt he had got to
the end of the road. He came because he felt he had got to
the beginning of the road, and I would say that the
church ought to be composed of people whose aim is to
find out more about Jesus and to match their lives with
what they find out.

Reid: But the church seems to be in decline today. Not
many people are interested. Why is that?

Barclay: Well, I am not prepared to accept this, as it were,
simpliciter. I don't think there is anything you can say
about the church which is true of the whole church. You
may be quite right that there are places in which the
church is in decline. I happen to live in a certain area of
Glasgow; if you began a couple of miles nearer the city
centre from where I live and proceed five or six miles out
beyond me you would get a whole series of churches
which are packed to the door. I think the trouble is that
the church has become a purely middle-class institution
and, in the middle-class areas, I don't think the church is
any weaker than ever it was, especially in the upper
middle-class areas. But I think that the church has
almost completely lost its place in the poorer areas and
what are left of the slum areas. Equally I think it has lost
its place at the top end of the social scale. This is the
trouble. I am not at all prepared to say this *simpliciter*
and without qualifications, that the church is on the way
down. I think it's very badly on the way down in certain
places, but not everywhere.

Reid: Why should it be losing out at the lower end and at the top end of the scale?

Barclay: I think it was always true that it was losing out at the top end of the scale and I think it is true because, at the top end of the scale, there are so many other things to do with a Sunday: the motor car, travel and all this kind of thing. Besides, I think it loses out at the top end of the scale simply because the richer you are, in a sense, the less you need your religion except when sorrow hits you or illness hits you or something like that. At the lower end of the social scale, you have got the interesting phenomenon that, when this section of our community changes its living place and goes into a new area of the city, it's there that the churches are strongest of all. It's the church-extension churches in Scotland which are supremely strong, crowded to the door. I think it's to be said that, when people can enter the church in a crowd, there's good hope. It's when individual people have to try to break into an established congregation that you do get difficulty in coming in. I would like new arrivals to remember that it's not so much that it's respectable people who make the church, it is just that the church makes people respectable—the other way round!

If I were dictator, which God forbid, I think I would try to do two things. I think, in one sense, I would abolish church membership. I never could forget, when I was dispensing the sacrament, that Jesus said, 'Him that comes unto me, I will in no way cast out.' It was an open door. In another sense, I would make a kind of membership of the Church which was open only to those who were fully and totally committed to it, and I would discipline that membership. I mean, if a person fell below his promise, I would discipline him there and then. I would cut the alleged church membership down by nine-

tenths, but what I had left would be totally and
absolutely committed. For the rest, the door would be
wide open for anyone who wanted to come.

Reid: I think you are referring to the Church of Scotland
practice of only allowing members to come to Communion. I mean, in my church, the United Reformed
Church, all are welcome at the Table whether they are
church members or not. But the idea of reducing the
numbers I can see has a certain appeal because probably
the average quality of church member is not very high,
the average amount of commitment being pretty low.

Barclay: Yes, it is as it were reducing 100% membership
but leaving the door wide open to other kinds of membership. But I am not at all sure of the wisdom of allowing
people to the communion table with no kind of prepara-
tion at all. If you do that, you have reduced the communion to pure magic. It seems to me that a man must know
what he is doing or there is not much value in his being
there.

Reid: It is interesting you should say this because, although
I was at one time an elder of the United Reformed
Church, I am a former Presbyterian and I have never
been entirely happy with the idea that just anyone can
come to Communion. There was always a certain appeal
in the Scottish Presbyterian idea that you had to be a
committed member.

Barclay: I don't so much want you to be a committed
member as I would want people to know what they are
doing.

Reid: Of course, the invitation which we put out is to all
those who love our Lord. That is the invitation. We don't
have an examination which they've got to pass.

Barclay: Yes, but at the same time, there is no doubt at all
that the early church had a colossal advantage over us
because the early church lived in a totally sacramental
age. The main feature of religion in early church days
came from the mystery religions. The mystery religions
were all passion-plays which told with music and incense
and lighting the story of a dying and rising God; this was
played out for the people, the greatest emotional urges
being applied, and the people were supposed to identify
with the dying and rising God. Now this kind of sacra-
mentalism is totally removed from modern ideas
altogether and from modern experience. In the ancient
world, they would immediately see how the bread and
the wine stand for the body and blood of Jesus Christ.
But I think that twentieth-century man needs an explanation with regard to this. You see, not to draw red herrings
and not to be controversial, the person who sits at Communion has to make up his mind whether, like the
Roman Catholics, he is actually eating and drinking the
body and the blood of Christ or whether, like the Pres-
byterians, he is handling something which represents the
body and blood of Christ but is not really that unless it be
accepted in faith. I would think something of this needs
to be explained.

Actually, in Scotland, one of the great discussions just
now is child-communion, and there is a strong move to
allow the child to come to communion.

Reid: What do you feel about that?

Barclay: If you ask me in theory, I would say I was totally
against it for the same reason that I have just given. I
would think that he who sits at the table must be not so
much a committed Christian as an instructed Christian
which isn't necessarily the same thing. On the other
hand, when I ran my Summer Institute for Americans in

St Andrews between 1969 and 1976, the closing act
was always a communion service at which even babies
were present, and at which I have seen people of thir-
teen and fourteen dispensing the elements. Although,
theoretically, I found it wrong, experientially I found it
most moving and think it might well be something worth
developing. But it's one thing doing this in a group of
people who have lived together, eaten together, laughed
together and studied together for three weeks. It is
another thing entirely doing it in a group of complete
strangers. I mean, in the three weeks something has been
built up which will stand this, but I doubt if in congrega-
tions of fourteen or fifteen hundred you can get this
build-up.

Reid: But to many people, I think there's a great irrelevance
about church service, and I often feel this myself. I sometimes sit there and I ask myself, 'What am I sitting here
for?' We've sung a few hymns, we've had a prayer, the
minister has read a couple of lessons, we've had an
anthem and then the minister stands up and preaches his
sermon. And sometimes I say, 'Is this the best I can be
doing with this hour on a Sunday? What is its
relevance?'

Barclay: I think you've got something here and I think if
ever we're going to get the lost people back in—I don't
mean lost in the theological sense—if we're ever going to
get the church's lost members back in, we've got to
remake our whole church order of service. Not, I think,
the morning service, because I think it's probably here to
remain. In the church where I'm an elder, every second
or third winter, in the evening services we take big
subjects, Christianity and money, Christianity and sex,
Christianity and law, Christianity and society, and we
invite the whole parish to come. We live in a parish of

about 2,000 houses, which is a manageable unit, and they're all buying their houses in instalments. I mean, it is a rather middle-class society. Now, we don't have any hymns or prayers at all. We have a two-sentence prayer and then we just go straight into a forty-five minute lecture. We then break and go down to the hall for coffee, and those who wish can stay to talk it over. Three to four hundred may come to this on a nasty winter evening, and anything from 120 to 150 will wait to talk; at 10 o'clock, we've to try to push them out. We finish with a proper epilogue—a really religious epilogue. We get all kinds of people: politically-motivated people, communists, socialists, nationalists, all this, who come for the argument, and I think there is something intensely valuable about it. But, if you get these people in and confront them with four singings, two scripture lessons and two prayers before you say anything to them, you lose them. I think the idea is to get them in and jump on them straight away and hope, as the years go on, you will build up the ability to worship. That's why I think the morning service should be kept much the way it is, because I would say it's the service for the mature Christian. The evening service is the service for the parish. I started in 1933 and I stopped in 1947 as far as the parish ministry was concerned, but if I were starting again, I would certainly in the summer attempt to take the church out to the people rather than wait for them to come to me. I wouldn't, I think, start preaching on the street corner. I can see modern difficulties in this straight away, but what I would do would be to say to the Golf Club, 'Would you mind if I have an epilogue in the bar at 10 o'clock at night?' Now, I think there would be a real welcome for this, especially if you played as much golf as I used to play and they knew you. I think Jesus could have done this with no trouble at all. In fact, I think it is the kind of thing he would have enjoyed doing.

Reid: What would the object of this be? Just to convert more people?

Barclay: The object of it is, in the first place, to remind people there is such a person as God, that there is something more than the game of golf and business and drink. The object would be, ultimately, that you would hope they would come to church. But not necessarily. As far as I can see, Jesus didn't try to sweep people into the Synagogue.

Reid: I think this is a very good idea.

Barclay: It could only happen in the kind of town I was a minister in. I was a minister in Renfrew which in those days had a population of about 14,000; everyone literally knew you and you knew everyone at least by sight. Your golf course was also the town club but, with a bit of imagination, I think it could be worked in most places.

Reid: Who is it who gives the lectures at your church at the moment, these forty-five-minute lectures?

Barclay: My minister and I share it. I did a good bit of it when I was well enough to do it and he does a good bit of it yet; we've also had the Chief of Police in to talk about law, a well known doctor and surgeon to talk about medicine and Christianity, and so on. We have also gone out for local people, people from Glasgow and people well known to the citizenry. We do not try to make people worship, in the normal sense of hymns and prayers and so on. We try to bring them face to face with Christian truth.

Reid: I wouldn't really interpret worship as hymns and prayers and sermons. That's maybe my difficulty. I think worship somehow or other is to surrender yourself to God, to allow God to work within you. I don't quite know that all these other things are necessary.

Barclay: I think you may well be right; at the same time, I think we have a certain number of older people whose foundations you would shake very badly if you didn't have a more-or-less conventional morning service. But I would certainly keep the evening for doing the kind of thing I am talking about.

Reid: What is worship then? How would you define worship?

Barclay: I would say that worship is anything that makes me aware of God and, for myself when I was in Renfrew, worship was listening every Saturday night to what was then the Scottish Orchestra. Music was worship. I can quite see that for some cricket or football might be worship at a particular time, but I think that there is something to be said for the conventional form of worship for the mature Christian who knows the hymns, who knows what prayer is all about and who is prepared to come into a group and be one of a group.

Reid: What is God's part in the service of worship then?

Barclay: Well, I have often been very angry at the opening prayer of a service when the preacher says something like, 'Come and be with us, O God, for this hour of worship', because I don't believe you can keep God out. God's part in worship, if you want, is simply that he's there. And our part in worship is to become aware that he's there.

Reid: Now this is something I prickle at a bit too, if the elder who gives the little prayer in the vestry before the service says, 'Now that we are about to come into your

presence, God'. I feel that God is with us every moment
of every day.

Barclay: I would agree strongly with this.

Reid: What do you think about the charismatic movement
that is entering into several churches? A big church near
me is split right down the middle because half of the
people want to bring this charismatic experience into the
service, and the other half don't.

Barclay: It depends what you mean by the word
'charismatic'. A charisma in Greek, and in the New
Testament, is a gift which you have, not by education
and not by training, but simply because of some kind of
special favour of God. This is not in the least mysterious.
You and I could both practise golf for twenty-five years,
sixteen hours a day, but we wouldn't be Gary Player.
Gary has a charisma for playing golf. Similarly, we
could practise, say, on a piano or a violin, but we
wouldn't be great exponents because we haven't got this
original charisma. So there's not anything particularly
unusual about this. There's not even anything particularly religious about it.

In the New Testament, church administration was a
charisma, healing was a charisma, all kinds of things
were a charisma but, in the modern charismatic
movement, you have two particular things. You have
healing, which at the moment we'll leave on one side
because we may be talking about it in another connection, and you have speaking with tongues. Now
speaking with tongues is dealt with by Paul in
I Corinthians 14; Paul's main attitude to this charisma
was that it existed all right but it was a nuisance, and he
says quite clearly he would rather speak half a dozen
words that people could understand than ten thousand
words in an unknown tongue. He doesn't deny that there

is such a thing as speaking with tongues. He says he's got the gift himself, but he does not regard it as nearly as important as the charismatics regard it. Paul would have said that speaking with tongues is not an entirely good thing because it may edify the person who's speaking but it doesn't edify the congregation.

Now I find this true. I find there are people who tell me that they speak with tongues and they get a marvellous feeling of relaxation and serenity and peace, but nobody has understood a word of what they are talking about. Now, I'm of the opinion that the charismatic movement has a big thing if they would insist that every gift in church is a charisma, that even the gift of a man who is able to work with electricity is a charisma. If only they wouldn't place such weight on what I would regard as a mere side-issue, this business of speaking with tongues.

Reid: Is there a sense in which the Church needs to decide on a basic message, as C. H. Dodd put it, the *kerygma*?

Barclay: The *kerygma* literally means a herald's announcement. The Greek for herald is *kerux* and his announcement is his *kerygma*, and the word was more or less introduced to England by C. H. Dodd. Now Dodd said that, in the speeches, and the sermons in *Acts* and in the Pauline letters, you have a basic message in which certain elements always occur. For instance: the time has come—Jesus has come—his life, death and resurrection are all the fulfilment of prophesy; he will come again to judge the quick and the dead; therefore, repent and receive the grace of God, or else be damned. It ends with a threat. This, I think, is the *kerygma*. There's a lot to be said, I think, for going back to this and, if not taking exactly this, of deciding what is the very centre of Christianity so that we preach it.

Reid: That is why I raised it because it seems to me that

Dodd was suggesting a basic message for the Christian church.

Barclay: I think there's still a basic message although I think the message would be a bit different from what it was in the first century.

Reid: I think he suggested that the centre of the message was that here was a man who went about doing good.

Barclay: Yes, that's it.

Reid: What is a Christian?

Barclay: A Christian, I would say, is a man who accepts the claims of Jesus Christ.

Reid: You see, I have a feeling that a man could be a Christian without having heard of Jesus Christ inasmuch as he lived a life according to the principles Jesus Christ laid down. He loves his neighbour and he loves God. In other words, he acts out the Christian ethic in his life. Is that not valid?

Barclay: I don't like it because it could be interpreted as being kind to Granny and the cat. It seems to me that there's something much deeper than just conduct in this. I think really the only man who got what Christianity was all about was Paul. He got it in that phrase which should be dear to you and me who are Scots: 'justification by faith'. Now justification by faith does not mean to make you good and to make you just. The Greek word to justify is *dikaioun*, and all Greek verbs which end in *oun* mean, not to make a person something; they mean to treat, reckon or account somebody as something. So the point about justification by faith is that, hell-deserving sinner though I certainly am, God regards me as if I were a beloved son. In other words, the essence of justification by faith is the parable of the prodigal son. He's a dirty little rascal but he went out a son and he comes back a son. I would say the essence of Christianity is that Jesus Christ came to demonstrate to me that, even though I'm a hell-deserving sinner, God still loves me.

Now you may say this makes things far too easy. But I don't think it does. It doesn't make things easy at all. If I owe the Income Tax Inspector something, and I write a cheque and pay it, so long as there are funds in the bank I've finished with him. He can't get another single thing from me. But, if I love someone, I'd give them the sun, the moon and the stars, and that wouldn't be enough. And again, suppose I drive my car under the influence, and I knock down a child, I am taken to court and I'm tried and I'm found guilty. I may have my licence suspended, I may be heavily fined, I may be sent to prison. But, once I've served my sentence, once the suspension time is finished, once I've paid the fine, the law has no claim on me whatever. I'm finished. But can I ever make it up to the mother of the child I killed? I can satisfy the law but I can't satisfy love. And that is why, if I say the whole essence of Christianity is that Jesus taught me that, hell-deserving sinner though I am, God loves me, I am left for the rest of my life trying to deserve that love. And that's where your Christian ethic comes in. I would say it doesn't come in in the first place, it comes in in the second place.

'Life After Death'

Reid: THE BIG attraction of the church is the hope it gives of life after death. Do you think that is a valid hope?

Barclay: I might have thought that once. I am not sure now. I have a vivid recollection of an extra-mural university class where I talked about the Christian beliefs and the Creed. When I came to the one about, 'I believe in the life everlasting', a middle-aged, talented, capable, efficient, handsome woman expressed the opinion that the last thing in the world that she wanted was immortality of any kind. She wanted to pass out because she was tired. Now I think quite a number of people in the modern world would quite gladly finish with everything. We live in an age of stress and strain and tension and quite a number of people would quite gladly just sleep eternity away. I'm sure this is the case.

Reid: But there are also an awful lot for whom that would seem like the end of all hope. Life would be meaningless if life didn't continue.

Barclay: Well, I'd better be completely honest in the start of the discussion. I don't disbelieve in the life to come but I've never been able to believe in it without any doubts, without any waverings, and without any hesitations at all. I've always wondered about this, but I would want to say with the utmost conviction that I've got that: if there is a life to come or if there is not a life to come, I would still regard the Christian way of life as the best whether there's any afterwards or not. I wouldn't myself at all either feel swindled or feel that life was purposeless if all that I had to hope for was this life.

Reid: Are there not, though, in the Bible indications that there will be a life to come?

Barclay: Yes, there are indications of this unquestionably, especially in the New Testament. But the Old Testament did not believe in a life to come. At least it didn't believe in any recognisable life to come. It believed in a grey, shadowy, colourless land where everyone went, good and bad alike, and where they were separated both from man and God—a place called Sheol, where people were shades rather than human beings. In the Old Testament there's very, very little belief in a life to come but not so in the New Testament. The New Testament is almost based on the assumption that there is a life to come. But I also think it's true to say that you can't really get any one kind of belief out of the New Testament. For instance, Jesus says, 'Today thou shalt be with me in Paradise,' as if the life to come began the moment you died. On the other hand, you get the belief that there's going to be a long sleep of a thousand years and, in that thousand years, the martyrs will rise at once but the ordinary people will not rise until the end of the thousand years. If Jesus was able to say, 'Today thou shalt be with me in Paradise', it indicated not only that the life to come began the minute you died, but also that in some way judgment was completed the minute you died too; whereas elsewhere the idea emerges that there's a sleep of a thousand years preceding the judgment. So I don't think you can get from the New Testament an accurate, complete picture, so to speak, of the life to come. On the other hand I think that the New Testament quite definitely does teach a life to come and looks at the living of life on earth, on the basis that there is a life to come.

Reid: Yet this is one part of the New Testament on which you have quite a bit of doubt. You've already said so, haven't you?

Barclay: No, I want to be fair to myself. I wouldn't so much regard it as having a bit of doubt as just not having certainty.

Reid: All right, I can accept that, but can you therefore have certainty in other bits of the New Testament?

Barclay: Oh, surely. I can be perfectly sure of God's attitude to me and my attitude to God without thinking in terms of other than this life, without really colliding with Christian belief. I can quite easily prove by logic that there is a life to come and I don't have any difficulty about this.

Reid: Can you do it in a way that I would understand it?

Barclay: Yes, I think so. We can argue that there's a life to come because of the justice of God. In this world, the best people—the martyrs—die in agony, dying for the sake of God. If all they got out of their love of God was an agony, then there's a definite injustice in this. I think that it's possible to argue that, in sheer defence of the justice of God, you have to argue for a life to come.

   I think it's also true that you can argue the life to come from the love of God. In this life, as we all know, it happens again and again that somebody dies young—in the human sense of the term, far too young; they have never developed, never done what they could have done, never been what they might have been. In the love of God, surely these people must have a chance to have and be and develop all the things that they have never been able to encompass in life.

I think, too, you can argue it from the nature of man. I mean, man's life is a continual development. At first, it's a physical and a mental development at the same time; then it becomes a spiritual development. You don't stop developing however old you are. As it were, you come closer and closer to God and nearer and nearer to spiritual things: I think it's fair to ask, 'Is all this development for nothing? Is it just to be cut off?' And I should think that in all logic the answer must be no. I think these are good arguments that there is a life to come.

Reid: If there were no life to come and you believed in the judgment of God, I think you would therefore have to be saying that we are judged every minute of the day?

Barclay: I do say that. In John's Gospel, Jesus says two things. He says, 'I came not to judge the world' and also he says, 'For judgment came I into the world'. And I think the point is this, that Jesus did not come to judge the world, but confrontation with Jesus is in itself an inevitable judgment. You confront a man with a great person or with a great experience and, if this person or this experience means nothing to him, he has exercised judgment on himself. The best example, the best analogy, is one that I've used often in writing and speaking. Suppose I, as in fact I do, find great delight in fine orchestral music. Suppose I have a friend who to my knowledge has never experienced orchestral music; then suppose I take this man to an orchestral concert with a view to giving him a new and splendid experience in life; and finally suppose the concert has hardly started before he is fidgeting and coughing and playing with caramel papers. All he has done is to demonstrate to me that he is a man with no music in his soul. I took him to give him what I regard as one of life's great experiences, and he condemned himself in the face of that experience. Now I

think it is the same with Jesus. When a man is confronted
with Jesus, that is a judgment. He has passed an act of
judgment. Jesus said that those who believe in him have
already passed from death to life. The judgment you pass
is as follows: if your heart goes out to Jesus, if you see in
him the finest person in the world, if you're moved to
love, then it's all right. But if you're left in indifference or
moved to dislike, then it's all wrong. Confrontation is
judgment.

Reid: I've often thought this about death, that it is frightening because we don't know what it is. But I've often felt it
must in a sense be like the child who is about to be born.
If this child is aware of where it is and is aware that it is to
be changed into some different kind of being or non-
being, it would be an equally frightening experience, and
death might just be like that—a change of situation
almost.

Barclay: I don't think many people are afraid of death.
I think almost everyone is afraid of dying. This is a
different thing altogether. Dying can be a messy, painful
and humiliating business. It's not death they're afraid of,
it's the process of dying. I mean, if everyone could die
instantly and painlessly, then I don't think anyone would
be afraid of death at all. It's the process that people are
afraid of.

I would like to make a point now which I didn't make
when I was giving the arguments in favour of the life to
come.

It is the argument which would convince me in the end
if I were to be fully convinced. I'm a universalist, an unre-
pentant universalist. I think that in the end everyone will
be saved. But, if I'm a universalist, I need other lives than
this in order that people may still be acted on by grace
and the mercy of God. I'm a universalist because the
Bible has a number of significant 'alls'. Jesus said, 'I, if I

be lifted up, will draw *all* men unto me' (*John* 12:32). In *1 Timothy*, he talks about God who desires *all* men to be saved (*1 Timothy* 2:4–6). Paul speaks in *Romans* about God who confined *all* men under sin that he might have mercy on all (*Romans* 3:3ff). And my view has always been that if, at the end of the day, there is one man left out, that man has defeated God, and this I just cannot believe possible. Again, if I thought of God as King, and if I thought of God as Judge primarily, then I suppose I could be quite willing to think of God as keeping his people under the punishment of hellfire or annihilating them or obliterating them. But I don't think of God primarily as King or Judge, I think of God primarily as Father and I cannot imagine any father being happy when millions of his children were frying in hell. This I just can't believe. And, lastly, I think that punishment is immoral unless punishment is such that it cures the person. All punishment must be curative. That, incidentally, is, I think, what is wrong with much of our present prison system. The present prison system is mere vengeance, retribution without thought of turning out the man better than he was. Therefore, I am a universalist who believes in hell. I think it may be necessary for a man to go to heaven *via* hell. He may have to be punished. But the punishment will be to correct him and to cure him and, in the end, to bring him to the love of God. I think God is such that there can be no world, no universe, no time in which his grace is not active to the end of time. And so, if I have to believe in universal salvation, I think I would need to believe in other lives in order to make this come true.

Reid: The Buddhists believe in other lives, don't they? They believe in reincarnation. That's not what you're talking about, is it?

Barclay: If I know Buddhists correctly, their reincarnation
is reincarnation as animals, is it not? No, I'm not
thinking of that at all, and I'm not thinking of coming
back to this life. I'm thinking of life in some other state of
being.

Reid: I think we must now, at this stage, have from you a
definition of heaven and a definition of hell.

Barclay: No, you don't. At least, I can't give you any definition of heaven and any definition of hell.

Reid: Yet, you've used the terms.

Barclay: I use the terms but I simply regard as hell that
punishment which God, being God, will mete out to his
people for their ultimate salvation. Heaven I simply
regard as the perfect blessedness which comes from
complete union with, and complete submission to, God.

Reid: Do you dismiss completely the old idea of heaven and
hell as being places?

Barclay: Well, I don't know. This is exactly what moves me
to doubts. You see, I do not so much doubt the life to
come, but I become distressed and amazed and
uncomprehending at the kind of pictures people try to
draw of the life to come. I obviously can't understand
God fully because I'm a human being, and, if I could
fully understand him, he wouldn't be God. Similarly, I
can't tell what's going to happen after I die. One of the
complaints I've got against spiritualists is that they will
draw you pictures of people having a good smoke and
this kind of thing. Well, if heaven is just an extension of
this world, I don't want it. It must be something different.

Reid: That indicates a certain disenchantment with this
world.

Barclay: No, not necessarily, but it's just that, however enchanted I may be with this world, if I'm going to live on, I don't want a repeat performance. I want something greater, bigger, better, nearer God than I am here.

Reid: I suppose though, that as a parish priest, you've had to face up to this problem of death, and would I be right in thinking that the only consolation that people normally have is the thought that there's a life to come?

Barclay: I think this is true. I've never had any interest in questions like, 'Will we know each other after death?' I think, on the whole, I would rather not because, if we know each other after death, I am not only going to meet the people I love; I'm going to meet the people I was disloyal to, for example. I think you've got to think in terms of a completely new world altogether. You see, as a parish minister, most of the deaths I attended were of old persons who were suffering a severe illness and, on the whole, most people were relieved and glad to see death come, for it was a release rather than a taking away. So, I wouldn't know what to answer to your question.

Reid: What is the Christian word of comfort to the mother or father who has lost a child?

Barclay: It depends. One thing the Christian must never say is that it's the will of God. I mean, for a child to die of some disease, is the last thing that God would want. The Christian word of comfort in that kind of case is, 'God is just as sorry as you are and if you ask him to help you, he'll give you strength and courage to get through this. But the best way you can get through it is simply to go on with life.' This, I think, is the Christian answer.

Discussion Seven

'Healing'

Reid: IN THE old days, as you said in one of our earlier discussions (see p. 9), people used to believe that illness and disease were connected with sin, and I suppose the psychologists might go along that road a bit today. What do you feel about that?

Barclay: I would certainly go along the road. I think that all suffering is connected with someone's misdoing. I wouldn't say it was sin in the popular sense of the term, but somebody's mistake, somebody's mistreatment of a situation or of a person. I think that all suffering is brought about like that. The difference I would make is that I wouldn't for one moment say that it's necessarily the afflicted person's mistake which has caused that suffering. It might be the parents, it might be the grandparents. I think it might be something like that. We are all, as the wonderful phrase in the Bible puts it, 'bound up in the bundle of life', and no man is an island. We are so bound up that if you say that suffering and disease are caused by someone's misdoings, it's not the person who suffers who's necessarily to blame. It may be somebody else altogether.

Reid: But, can you apply that to someone who, for example, gets an infectious disease, a serious infectious disease?

Barclay: Well, there are two answers to that. The first is quite simply, we can't blame God for what the man might well have escaped. If he, with his eyes open, goes into an infected area, he can't blame God if he gets an infectious disease. Secondly, I believe the infectious disease is the cause of someone's misdoing in some way or another.

Reid: Are you able to elaborate on that? Or is it just a feeling you have?

Barclay: No, the Bible's view is that, if Adam hadn't sinned, the chances are immortality would have been the lot of everyone. I think that all ills could ultimately be traced to some misuse of the body, not necessarily by the patient but by someone who has something to do with him.

Reid: One of his ancestors, you mean?

Barclay: Oh yes, someone who went before him, that's right.

Reid: Is this tied up at all with the old idea of the sins of the fathers being visited upon those who follow them?

Barclay: It certainly is. There are many, many terrible diseases which are transmittable. They don't stop with the parent, they go on to the child. This is absolutely true.

Reid: What is the Christian role in the healing of the body, in medicine, in health generally?

Barclay: Well, I think the Christian role is just healing. Do you mean, apart from the doctor?

Reid: No, I mean, does the church, for example, have a role to play in the healing of sickness? I mean, the old church used to be a healing church but, in the main, there are very few healing churches now.

Barclay: You're bringing up the large question of spiritual healing and I think the question of spiritual healing is just this; according to John, Jesus said, 'Things that I do now, you will do these same things and greater things too'. This simply meant that men would discover things and so they would be able to carry out by medical scientific methods the healings Jesus did. I would think this will become truer as we learn more about the control of diseases. I would say the church's place in regard to healing is not herself to try to heal, but to bring to people the serenity and peace of mind which will make healing easier and more certain by ordinary medical means.

Reid: Can we then, now that we've got on to this subject, say a little bit about Jesus' healing and what you think happened? How did he work?

Barclay: Well, I think in the first place that if a person is like Jesus, perfectly submitting to the will of God, I think that that person can both acquire and be given powers that the ordinary person could never have. I think if the power of working miracles was given to people like you or me, we would almost certainly do a great deal more harm than good with it. You've got to be a certain kind of person before this can develop within you and before it can be given to you.

Secondly, I would say that I think a great many of Jesus' miracles are explicable by modern scientific methods. For instance, demon possession. I don't believe there's any such thing as demon possession because I don't believe there are such beings as demons, but the people involved had got it firmly into their heads that they were possessed; and you can only cure a person by assuming the reality of his illness. If you've got a well-loved, well-trusted doctor, the minute that doctor enters the room your blood pressure goes down and your temperature goes down. You've got, in his presence, a confidence that you certainly don't have when he's not there. Suppose you raise this to the nth power and you get Jesus' impact and his personality on someone who is ill psychologically!

Thirdly, in Palestine, the Jews actually believed that no-one was ever ill unless he had sinned. This had a psychological effect on people. Once people had the idea they had sinned, they might then go on to get, for example, paralysis of a limb—as a result of a psychological condition. You will remember that when Jesus faced the man let down through the roof by the four friends, his first words were, 'Your sins are forgiven'. This was necessary. The effect of the mind on the body is incalculable.

There's a man called Tournier who writes a series of medical books, notably *A Doctor's Case Book*, in the light of the New Testament. He tells the story of a girl who was a patient of a friend of his and who had a blood count in pernicious anaemia such as was bound to be fatal. So he got her removed to a sanatorium in Switzerland. In a short time, he telephoned to ask how she was and he was told she was very much better, but that her blood count was never anything like what he had said it was.

Now, he knew his laboratory methods were good and he knew his technique was right so he got in touch with the girl and said to her, 'I'm glad you're better. I'm glad your blood count is as good as it is. Has anything happened to you since I was dealing with you and we got the terribly bad blood count?'

'Well,' she said, after thinking a while, 'just one thing has happened to me. I had a terrible, bitter grudge against an old friend, and suddenly I found myself able to forgive. From that moment, I felt better'.

Her psychological or spiritual condition had actually affected her blood count. Now, Jesus knew this and Jesus, I think, worked by the impact of his personality on the other person. I think most of the things Jesus cured were, to use the modern jargon, psychosomatic. They were bodily conditions produced by a spiritual condition.

Reid: So there we have a good example for our own lives. It is to forgive, isn't it?

Barclay: Absolutely. It couldn't be clearer. You would get rid of a lot of your illnesses if you would just clear things up with your fellow men.

Reid: I think all of us have really experienced this in our lives, haven't we?

Barclay: One way or another, yes.

Reid: And yet it is an experience which doesn't always lead us on to the next forgiveness.

Barclay: As it should, that's right.

Reid: I want to ask you next about the nature miracles as I think you call them but, as it is such a big subject, perhaps we ought to leave it for another day.

Barclay: Yes, another day ...

POST SCRIPT: But, to my sorrow, there was not to be another day. Death claimed William Barclay in January 1978 and so this book was never completed.

Iain Reid.